MIKE BARTLETT

Mike Bartlett's plays include *King Charles III* (Almeida/West End); *An Intervention* (Paines Plough/Watford Palace Theatre); *Bull* (Sheffield Theatres/Off-Broadway); *Medea* (Glasgow Citizens/Headlong); *Chariots of Fire* (based on the film; Hampstead/West End); *13* (National Theatre); *Love, Love, Love* (Paines Plough/Plymouth Drum/Royal Court); *Earthquakes in London* (Headlong/National Theatre); *Cock* (Royal Court/Off-Broadway); *Artefacts* (Nabokov/Bush); *Contractions* and *My Child* (Royal Court).

He was Writer-in-Residence at the National Theatre in 2011, and the Pearson Playwright-in-Residence at the Royal Court Theatre in 2007. *Cock* won an Olivier Award for Outstanding Achievement in an Affiliate Theatre in 2010. *Love, Love, Love* won the TMA Best New Play Award in 2011. *Bull* won the same award in 2013. *King Charles III* won the Critics' Circle Award for Best New Play in 2015.

Directing credits include *Medea* (Glasgow Citizens/Headlong); *Honest* (Northampton Royal & Derngate) and *Class* (Tristan Bates).

He has written seven plays for BBC Radio, winning the Writers' Guild Tinniswood and Imison prizes for *Not Talking*, and his three-part television series, *The Town*, was broadcast on ITV1 in 2012 and nominated for a BAFTA for Breakthrough Talent.

He is currently developing television projects with the BBC, ITV, Big Talk, and Drama Republic, and under commission from Headlong Theatre, Liverpool Everyman and Playhouse, Hampstead Theatre, and the Royal Court Theatre.

Other Titles in this Series

Mike Bartlett
BULL
AN INTERVENTION
KING CHARLES III

Tom Basden
HOLES
JOSEPH K
THERE IS A WAR

Jez Butterworth
JERUSALEM
JEZ BUTTERWORTH PLAYS: ONE
MOJO
THE NIGHT HERON
PARLOUR SONG
THE RIVER
THE WINTERLING

Caryl Churchill
BLUE HEART
CHURCHILL PLAYS: THREE
CHURCHILL PLAYS: FOUR
CHURCHILL: SHORTS
CLOUD NINE
DING DONG THE WICKED
A DREAM PLAY *after* Strindberg
DRUNK ENOUGH TO SAY
     I LOVE YOU?
FAR AWAY
HOTEL
ICECREAM
LIGHT SHINING IN
     BUCKINGHAMSHIRE
LOVE AND INFORMATION
MAD FOREST
A NUMBER
SEVEN JEWISH CHILDREN
THE SKRIKER
THIS IS A CHAIR
THYESTES *after* Seneca
TRAPS

Stella Feehily
BANG BANG BANG
DREAMS OF VIOLENCE
DUCK
O GO MY MAN
THIS MAY HURT A BIT

debbie tucker green
BORN BAD
DIRTY BUTTERFLY
NUT
RANDOM
STONING MARY
TRADE & GENERATIONS
TRUTH AND RECONCILIATION

Nancy Harris
LOVE IN A GLASS JAR
NO ROMANCE
OUR NEW GIRL

Rose Heiney
ELEPHANTS

Vicky Jones
THE ONE

Dawn King
CIPHERS
FOXFINDER

Lucy Kirkwood
BEAUTY AND THE BEAST
     with Katie Mitchell
BLOODY WIMMIN
CHIMERICA
HEDDA *after* Ibsen
IT FELT EMPTY WHEN THE
     HEART WENT AT FIRST BUT
     IT IS ALRIGHT NOW
NSFW
TINDERBOX

Conor McPherson
DUBLIN CAROL
McPHERSON PLAYS: ONE
McPHERSON PLAYS: TWO
McPHERSON PLAYS: THREE
THE NIGHT ALIVE
PORT AUTHORITY
THE SEAFARER
SHINING CITY
THE VEIL
THE WEIR

Chloë Moss
CHRISTMAS IS MILES AWAY
HOW LOVE IS SPELT
FATAL LIGHT
THE GATEKEEPER
THE WAY HOME
THIS WIDE NIGHT

Bruce Norris
CLYBOURNE PARK
THE LOW ROAD
THE PAIN AND THE ITCH
PURPLE HEART

Jack Thorne
2ND MAY 1997
BUNNY
BURYING YOUR BROTHER IN THE
     PAVEMENT
HOPE
JACK THORNE PLAYS: ONE
LET THE RIGHT ONE IN
     after John Ajvide Lindqvist
MYDIDAE
STACY & FANNY AND FAGGOT
WHEN YOU CURE ME

Phoebe Waller-Bridge
FLEABAG

Enda Walsh
BALLYTURK
BEDBOUND & MISTERMAN
DELIRIUM
DISCO PIGS & SUCKING DUBLIN
ENDA WALSH PLAYS: ONE
ENDA WALSH PLAYS: TWO
MISTERMAN
THE NEW ELECTRIC BALLROOM
ONCE
PENELOPE
THE SMALL THINGS
THE WALWORTH FARCE

Tom Wells
JUMPERS FOR GOALPOSTS
THE KITCHEN SINK
ME, AS A PENGUIN

Mike Bartlett

GAME

NICK HERN BOOKS

London

www.nickhernbooks.co.uk

A Nick Hern Book

Game first published in Great Britain in 2015 as a paperback original by Nick Hern Books Limited, The Glasshouse, 49a Goldhawk Road, London W12 8QP

Game copyright © 2015 Mike Bartlett

Mike Bartlett has asserted his right to be identified as the author of this work

Cover image by Leo Warner for 59 Productions

Designed and typeset by Nick Hern Books, London
Printed in Great Britain by CPI Group (UK) Ltd

A CIP catalogue record for this book is available from the British Library

ISBN 978 1 84842 472 2

Game was first performed at the Almeida Theatre, London, on 23 February 2015, with the following cast:

BELLE	Georgina Beedle
LIAM	Oscar Bennett
FLORENCE/MARGARET	Clare Burt
JOHN/PAUL	Daniel Cerqueira
SOLDIER, *in projection*	Laurence Grant
DAVID	Kevin Harvey
MANDY	Chloe Hesar
CARLY	Jodie McNee
LIAM	Jonah Miller
ASHLEY	Mike Noble
SIMON	Ben Righton
LIAM	Ben Roberts
GARY	Richard Sumitro
SARAH/EMMA	Susan Wokoma

Director	Sacha Wares
Design	Miriam Buether
Costume Design	Alex Lowde
Lighting Design	Jack Knowles
Sound Design	Gareth Fry
Video Design	Leo Warner
	for 59 Productions
Movement Director	Leon Baugh
Casting	Julia Horan CDG
Assistant Director	Anthony Almeida
Costume Supervisors	Eleanor Dolan,
	Jemima Penny
Dialect Coach	Charmian Helen Hoare

Characters

ASHLEY
CARLY
JOHN
DAVID
GARY
SIMON
PAUL
FLORENCE
EMMA
MANDY
BELLE
LIAM
MARGARET
SARAH

An indentation of the dialogue means the characters are in the hide.

Blank space on the page means a pause of equivalent length.

(/) means the next speech begins at that point.

(–) means an interruption.

(…) at the end of a speech means it trails off. On its own, it indicates a pressure, expectation or desire to speak.

A speech with no written dialogue indicates a character deliberately remaining silent.

This text went to press before the end of rehearsals and so may differ slightly from the play as performed.

Scene One

CARLY *and* ASHLEY *are looking around the house.*

JOHN *is showing* DAVID *the hides.*

CARLY	Worktops are probably granite that's what they use. You think I can take pictures gonna show Fiona she'll be so pissed off. She asked me for the number so she can get in on it and I was like no way, not stealing my thunder.

Soft-close drawers.

Induction hob, you know what that is, you have to use special pans but they give you those. You need the loo or something?

ASHLEY   What?

CARLY   Distracted.

ASHLEY   Just looking.

JOHN   You excited?

DAVID   Yes.

JOHN   To see it?

DAVID   Absolutely.

JOHN   You don't look excited.

CARLY   It's a lot to take in I know.

ASHLEY   Yeah.

JOHN   Is it what you expected?

DAVID   I suppose... I had an idea from the description but...

JOHN	...but?
	What?
	Any comments? Thoughts?
DAVID	No. No.
JOHN	Is there anything you think we should improve?
DAVID	You mean... No. It all looks good.
JOHN	You'd be happy with it like this then?
DAVID	Is it finished?
JOHN	You tell me.
CARLY	Hot tub.
DAVID	Yeah. Looks good. I like it.
CARLY	You know what you're supposed to do in a hot tub?
ASHLEY	You mean –
CARLY	Yeah.
ASHLEY	But wouldn't they be...
CARLY	Not all the time. No.
ASHLEY	Okay.
JOHN	Wouldn't be everyone's cup of tea, stuck in here all day.
DAVID	I've done worse jobs.
JOHN	What?
DAVID	...you know. Cleaning up, slopping out.
JOHN	Cleaning? This isn't like that.
DAVID	I know

JOHN	This is skilled, we need people who are highly trained.
DAVID	I am
JOHN	Professional. David, you're here because we thought you had the relevant skills.
DAVID	I do.
JOHN	You do?
DAVID	I have the experience. The skills. Look. I really want this. I think I'd do it well.

    …

    DAVID *looks around. Trying to find something to say.*

    It's bigger than I thought.

    ASHLEY *looks over the fence.*

CARLY	What are you up to?
ASHLEY	Checking.
CARLY	What?
JOHN	'Bigger'.
	How much do you think we're charging? Not for the champagne, the extras. Just this. How much?
DAVID	Three hundred.
JOHN	Five. Five hundred.
DAVID	Right.
JOHN	Per shot.
DAVID	Yeah… well… that sounds…
JOHN	This isn't cheap.

DAVID	No.
JOHN	Sold out first two months already, and the clients, when they get here, they'll expect a safe, professional, five-star reception. This is distinctly high-end. You understand?
DAVID	Yes.
ASHLEY	It's in the middle of nowhere.
CARLY	We could go for walks in the country.
ASHLEY	Miles from the station.
CARLY	Oh you mean it's a bad thing.
JOHN	It's as much about hospitality yes?
ASHLEY	An hour from town on the bus, yeah, and they only come –
CARLY	We'd use the car.
ASHLEY	What car?
	We get the car?
CARLY	You get everything.
JOHN	There'll be all sorts, and when they come in, they've got to feel happy. They might want to chat. Banter. Or they might want to be left to it.
CARLY	You had a look in the bedroom?
	ASHLEY *goes upstairs, and looks in the rooms.*
JOHN	Either way you've got to stay in here with them, so you need to make quick judgements as to how to give them what they need.
DAVID	Fine.

JOHN	You've got to enjoy that side of it.
DAVID	Yeah, I would.
JOHN	Right.
	Because I noticed on your CV, you don't have any experience of that side of things, and forgive me, but right now? In this conversation? You seem rather... stilted.
DAVID	I'm fine. I'm relaxed.
JOHN	But I'm not. You know what I mean?
CARLY	You seen the bed?
	CARLY *goes upstairs and joins* ASHLEY *in the bedroom.*
DAVID	It... I suppose it might not be coming across. But when I'm relaxed I'm a talker. Trust me. Don't have a problem normally, normally can't shut me up so –
JOHN	It's more about listening.
	I would've thought.
	CARLY *and* ASHLEY *come out onto the landing.*
CARLY	Can't stay at Mum's much longer.
ASHLEY	That's true.
CARLY	Thought you were going to lose it the other day, her shoving the paper in your face, like you haven't been on the computer all morning for exactly that reason, trying to find –
ASHLEY	Yeah, yeah...
DAVID	Are they two of the –
JOHN	Might be. Up to them.

A moment. CARLY *and* ASHLEY *keep looking round.*

CARLY   You could have that room to watch your films in. Big screen, PS4 whatever it is.

ASHLEY   They give you that?

CARLY   Don't know. You get money. Not much. Enough. But yeah you'd have your own space. Or it's somewhere for the kids.

ASHLEY   Kids?

CARLY   What?

ASHLEY   I thought you – You never –

CARLY   Get one of those bunk-bed slides from Ikea, they'd love that, be happy. Paint the room a colour or something.

ASHLEY   Thought you didn't want them.

CARLY   Well I don't. Not as things stand, you've seen Fiona. Sponging off her sister, she's a mess, can't cope, we'd be like that. But this is different.

JOHN   So?

CARLY   Boy in there, girl there, everyone's happy.

JOHN   Any questions?

DAVID   Oh…

CARLY   Jack and Missy.

ASHLEY   *Jack and Missy?*

             ASHLEY *smiles and kisses* CARLY. *They walk back downstairs.*

DAVID   What are you going to use?

JOHN   We were thinking converted SA80s

DAVID	You're... Right.
JOHN	That was the advice we received. Standard issue apparently. Why? Got a better idea?
DAVID	...
JOHN	...
DAVID	L96. I mean, if that's the experience you're after. SA80's standard, but from what you're saying that's not what this is. Standard. Is it? If you're spending all this money, like you say, on this scale, you'd want to get it right.
JOHN	Interesting.
ASHLEY	We don't pay them anything, a deposit or –
CARLY	We just have to sign up.
	We just have to say yes.
	It's a big thing.
ASHLEY	What do you think?
CARLY	Don't know. Don't know.
JOHN	You're available to start next week?
DAVID	You're offering it?
JOHN	I am.
DAVID	What about the interview?
JOHN	That was it. Days are short. Lots to do.
DAVID	Thought it would be a thing round a table. Wore a suit.
JOHN	Open the box.

DAVID	What?
JOHN	There.

DAVID does. And takes out a sniper rifle.

Tell me what it is.

DAVID	L96
JOHN	Great minds.

David. You're just what we're looking for.

So… You're on board?

DAVID	I… Yeah. Yes. Thank you.

Thank you sir.

JOHN	You don't need to call me sir.

They look at each other – different worlds.

CARLY	The woman has to know by Monday.
ASHLEY	So we've got tomorrow.
CARLY	Tomorrow, yeah.

They look around.

Good though. Isn't it?

ASHLEY	Yeah. It is.

Smile at each other. Hold hands.

Scene Two

Two weeks later.

ASHLEY *and* CARLY *are in the hot tub, both holding glasses of Pimm's.*

DAVID *is in the hide with* GARY *and* SIMON, *watching them.*

GARY	(*Sniggers.*)

> *A moment.* CARLY *and* ASHLEY *relaxing.* ASHLEY *sips his drink.*
>
> (*Sniggers again.*)

SIMON	What?
CARLY	Asparagus is an aphrodisiac.
ASHLEY	What's that supposed to mean?
CARLY	Makes you horny.
ASHLEY	Yeah I know that, but why are you suddenly –
CARLY	It was on TV.
	I might wear some special underwear tonight.
ASHLEY	Why?
CARLY	Why what? Fun. Don't know.
ASHLEY	I don't need help.
CARLY	It's not help. It's spice.
ASHLEY	'Spice'?
CARLY	Taste the difference.
GARY	Look.
SIMON	Yeah.
GARY	Sipping it. Thinks he's – Just drink it! Fucking…
DAVID	You ever used a weapon before?

GARY	Yeah.
SIMON	No he hasn't.
GARY	Yeah. I have.
SIMON	Paintball.
GARY	Can you get him to move?
DAVID	The important thing is to put your foot back to brace yourself.
GARY	He's just lying there like a dick.
DAVID	Sorry?
GARY	You can't do anything?
DAVID	It's about patience.
	You've just got the one shot so make it count.
GARY	Make it count?
	Where do you think we are mate?
	Syria?

SIMON *laughs*.

CARLY	I'm getting a tan.
ASHLEY	Yeah you are.
CARLY	Like being on holiday.
ASHLEY	Yeah.

They kiss.

ASHLEY *laughs*.

GARY	How old is she?
DAVID	It says in the pack.
GARY	What?
DAVID	There.

SIMON	Right.

He looks.

CARLY	I could lie on top of you.
ASHLEY	You could.
CARLY	Make it difficult for them. I'll be your armour.

She tries, but it's ridiculous. They laugh.

GARY	So is this the first time?
DAVID	Yes.
GARY	How old is she?

CARLY gets off ASHLEY, and they settle back down.

SIMON	Carly.
GARY	What?
SIMON	Five foot six
	Nine stone
	Twenty-four years old.
GARY	Butterface.
SIMON	Yeah.
CARLY	By the doors, you know when the sun comes in, sometimes I... okay this is stupid... but sometimes I just stand there, with them open, the air coming in.
GARY	What do you think mate?
DAVID	I... don't...
CARLY	I want to get one of those flowery dresses.
GARY	You don't know what a butterface is?
DAVID	No.

CARLY	In Mum's flat I'd have looked stupid wearing a dress like that, get all sweaty, it would just stick to me.
GARY	Great body.
CARLY	Get coffee down it or something
GARY	Great figure, you know, legs, tits.
CARLY	But here
GARY	Everything's good
CARLY	You can just stand there and it's…
GARY	Everything's good but her face
SIMON	Butterface.

ASHLEY *shuts his eyes.*

CARLY *shuts her eyes.*

GARY	Do you think she'll cry?
SIMON	What?
GARY	If she's not used to it. When it's done.
	She might.
	If she does. Seriously If she cries, I might have to
SIMON	What?
GARY	Crack one off.
SIMON	Fuck's sake.
GARY	If she cries that's going to fucking turn me on.

ASHLEY *stands up.*

ASHLEY	Might get a beer.

CARLY	Ashley. Can I just say I'm ready? I'm so fucking fertile. I can feel all those chemicals swimming around my body know the time is right I'm different.
ASHLEY	Why are you talking about all that? When they're –
CARLY	What? I'm saying I'm good that's all. I'm just –

A loud sound, CARLY *jumps.* ASHLEY *is shot by* GARY *and falls to the ground immediately. The boys cheer, amazed.*

Fuck / fuck fuck.

GARY	You see him! / He was like…
SIMON	Fuck. You got him! You got him.

She goes over to him.

CARLY	Okay.
	Okay.
SIMON	Mate!
	/ Mate!
CARLY	Okay. Shit.
SIMON	Mate, look at her.
CARLY	Fuck.
GARY	Come on…

A moment.

Then she starts to cry. Stops herself.

SIMON	There.
GARY	Yeah.

She reaches for her watch. Checks the time.

CARLY   Fuck.

               Okay.

               She stands and waits.

DAVID   That's it then.

GARY   Yeah that was good. Really good.
                        Getting a loyalty card. You do those?

DAVID   Yes we do.

GARY   I'm getting one. You getting one?

SIMON   Yeah.

               CARLY *goes and gets a glass of water.*

DAVID   Alright then. Come on lads.

SIMON   'Come on lads'

DAVID   What?

SIMON   Nothing.

               They leave.

               CARLY *comes back and waits by* ASHLEY.

               DAVID *follows.*

Scene Three

Two months later.

ASHLEY *is watching TV. An action film.*

DAVID *is in the hide with* PAUL *and* FLORENCE.

FLORENCE	There were supposed to be two.
DAVID	There... are.
FLORENCE	There's not. Look I'll count them: one, one.
PAUL	Can you shut up?
DAVID	I meant you're right, there's supposed to be two. I don't know where she – she isn't normally – I can make a call... or – oh.

The front door opens and CARLY *comes in, carrying three carrier bags, full of shopping.*

CARLY	Hey
ASHLEY	How was it?
CARLY	Yeah. Okay. What's that?
ASHLEY	(*Standing.*) Doesn't matter.
CARLY	No you keep watching.

She goes through to the kitchen, and unpacks the shopping. ASHLEY *stays watching the television, but uncomfortably. He wants to speak to* CARLY.

FLORENCE	So he can go for her instead?
DAVID	Yes. If you pay for it.
FLORENCE	Oh. It's extra. I see.
PAUL	I'm fine. Don't want her. Just him.

CARLY   He checked everything, said I was doing
                 okay. What's good is when you go in there
                 you don't have to wait, it's clean, there's a
                 coffee machine, music, and magazines, like
                 Condé Nast, you know what that is?
                 Expensive holidays and stuff. It sounds weird
                 but here, going to the doctor is actually
                 alright.

ASHLEY   Good.

CARLY   And he's nice.

ASHLEY   Did he say why it happened?

CARLY   Just that it does. It's normal.

                 He switches the television off.

FLORENCE   How much is she?

DAVID   Five fifty.

PAUL   I told you –

FLORENCE   I can *speak* Paul, I am allowed to do
                         that.

CARLY   You don't have to.

ASHLEY   It's fine. It was rubbish.

                 She keeps on unpacking. ASHLEY *comes and
                 stands awkwardly near the kitchen.*

FLORENCE   Why is it more?

DAVID   We need to calibrate the dose more
                         precisely for the women so –

FLORENCE   Paul? What do you think?

PAUL   Told you what I think stupid bitch.

FLORENCE   Oh stop showing off.

ASHLEY   Got worried. You're a bit late.

CARLY	I went shopping after. Thought while I was out…
ASHLEY	Yeah. No. Good.
FLORENCE	So. Her. Yes or no?
PAUL	*No.*
ASHLEY	So he didn't talk about this at all?
CARLY	He said there's no specific reason, that he can tell, so we should… you know. Keep trying.
ASHLEY	You mean.
CARLY	Have another go.
FLORENCE	Wouldn't she be more fun?
PAUL	I don't care. Fine. Her then.
FLORENCE	Oh. Right. You do want her now?
ASHLEY	No specific reason.
CARLY	Right.
FLORENCE	Cos it's your *treat* you should have what you want.
PAUL	Shut up.
FLORENCE	We're supposed to be having *fun*.
PAUL	Yeah I would if you –
FLORENCE	We're supposed to be doing this together! It was my idea.
PAUL	Just take it off the card.
FLORENCE	Right. Take it off the card. You're going for her. Not a problem.
CARLY	He said lots of women have had babies, in the other houses.
ASHLEY	How many?

CARLY	I don't know. But he said 'lots' and he wouldn't lie –
ASHLEY	He's employed by them.
CARLY	He's a doctor.
ASHLEY	Yeah but –
CARLY	If I don't trust what he says then what's the point in going?
FLORENCE	You remember when you first fired a gun David?
DAVID	Yes.
FLORENCE	How did it feel?
DAVID	I enjoyed it.
FLORENCE	You're saying it made you feel more masculine?
DAVID	Well –
FLORENCE	More powerful. Primal.
DAVID	Maybe.
FLORENCE	You hearing this Paul?
ASHLEY	So he didn't say anything about the darts.
CARLY	He said there's absolutely no reason to think it was the darts.
ASHLEY	I just thought he might have checked with the company.
CARLY	He doesn't need to. There's a three-month cut-off, the warden's briefed, everything's in place to make it safe, and as he pointed out, it's very common to lose a baby, whoever you are, statistically it happens all the time.

A long pause.

FLORENCE	You know you're going for the *woman* now yes?
PAUL	Fuck off.
FLORENCE	Don't you fucking swear at me, it looked like you were going for the man.
PAUL	He keeps getting in the way.
DAVID	Just take your –

PAUL *fires the gun, but* CARLY *and* ASHLEY *remain standing. A moment, then –*

FLORENCE	Did you just miss? Did he just miss? Missed. Jesus Christ Paul. Bet that's never happened before. They're right there! Anyone ever missed before.
PAUL	Of course they have.
FLORENCE	Have they.
PAUL	Been going months.
FLORENCE	Have they?
DAVID	…well… no.
FLORENCE	Ha! See? Unique! You're uniquely useless.
CARLY	It happened to Fiona, twice, before she got pregnant so –
FLORENCE	Did we pay for that?
DAVID	You pay for the shot so –
FLORENCE	Fucking hell. Can we buy another one?
DAVID	Yes.
FLORENCE	Right. Give him another go.

DAVID *reloads the gun.*

DAVID   Just take your time. There's no rush.

FLORENCE   If I had a penny the number of times
                         I've told him that.

PAUL   He doesn't find you funny.

ASHLEY   Maybe you should call her. Fiona.

CARLY   Why?

ASHLEY   Invite her over.

CARLY   Why? No. Be weird. Don't speak in ages,
             then suddenly call her up. She won't come
             anyway. Too far.

ASHLEY   Might be good to talk to her. About it.

CARLY   No. I'm okay. Doctor said I'm good.

FLORENCE   He's not holding it right.

DAVID   He's doing fine.

CARLY and ASHLEY unpack.

PAUL shifts slightly.

PAUL   He's still in the way, I can't…

DAVID   Take your time.

A moment.

                         Give it a moment. She'll come to you.

*CARLY turns to say something a little more
positive to ASHLEY.*

*She smiles. Energy for the first time in the
scene.*

CARLY   Ashley…

DAVID   All yours.

ASHLEY turns to CARLY.

ASHLEY   What?

CARLY's about to speak, when PAUL *shoots*
her. She falls to the floor of the kitchen.

DAVID   Perfect.

PAUL   Yeah?

DAVID   It was good.

FLORENCE   Really? You think? Didn't look good.

ASHLEY kneels down to CARLY, *and slowly*
lifts her up and puts her on a chair.

Bit of a mess.

Paul?

ASHLEY goes to get a glass of water.

Paul, how did it feel?

ASHLEY goes to do the last bits of
unpacking, and finds, in the shopping, a tiny
Babygro, with cat's ears.

He looks at it. Then at CARLY.

PAUL   I want a fucking drink.

He goes.

FLORENCE   Oh. Oh. Right. Yeah. *Good!*

She goes.

DAVID looks through to ASHLEY, *holding*
the Babygro.

CARLY wakes up. Goes to ASHLEY, *and*
takes the water. Drinks.

Scene Four

Evening.

ASHLEY *is in the living room playing on an iPad. The lights are low.*

CARLY *is in her bedroom, sat on the bed.*

A moment.

She stands.

Looks in the mirror.

Three girls and DAVID *enter the booth.* EMMA*'s got the brochure.*

MANDY	Oh my god this is / weird.
EMMA	Shit you can see / right in.
BELLE	This was such a good idea.
MANDY	Is that her?
EMMA	'Carly'
BELLE	What's she / doing?
MANDY	Were you in the army?
DAVID	I used to be.

CARLY comes back out of her bedroom, stands on the mezzanine level.

MANDY	Yeah my brother's in the army. There's a way you walk. He's got it and you've got it. I noticed. See them in the clubs sometimes, all the army boys. They're fit but they're kids really aren't they, all the privates.
BELLE	Mandy shut up.
MANDY	I'm the birthday girl David. I'm Mandy.

DAVID	Hi.
MANDY	I'm taking the shots.
	She picks up the gun. CARLY *sits down on the stairs and starts peeling her fingernails.*
	How do you do it?
DAVID	You put the butt of the rifle into your shoulder...
MANDY	Can you show me?
DAVID	It goes... that's right. In there.
MANDY	In there?
BELLE	You're such a fucking slut / Mandy –
MANDY	Shut up.
DAVID	And then you put your foot back like –
BELLE	Urrrghh. Fuck's sake.
	Shit! You seen what she's doing?
	Urrrrgh look at her!
	Switch it off.
EMMA	Switch it off?
	You can't *switch it off*. It's *real*! *Ha!*
BELLE	I know but... / Urrrgh.
EMMA	'Switch it off'
BELLE	Look at her!
EMMA	Can they hear?
DAVID	No.
MANDY	Does she know we're watching?
BELLE	Yeah, they have times, times when they might –

DAVID	Not any more.
BELLE	Yeah it says it in the brochure so –
DAVID	It's changed. In response to demand. They don't know when it'll be, now.
BELLE	Reprint the brochure then?
MANDY	Shall I do it?
BELLE	No! You've got to stalk them.

CARLY *comes fully downstairs and stands by* ASHLEY.

CARLY	It's late.
ASHLEY	Yeah.
CARLY	
ASHLEY	
CARLY	?
ASHLEY	Yeah.

ASHLEY *turns off the iPad, but just sits there.*

MANDY	David? Will you tell me…
DAVID	Whenever it feels right.
MANDY	Nah, tell me your number?
	You've got nice arms.

They all laugh.

He looks away.

Aw.

Okay

Shut up now girls. Concentrate.

CARLY *sits down, on the arm of the sofa, next to* ASHLEY.

*She starts to unbutton her shirt. The girls in
the booth laugh.*

BELLE   What's she doing? I don't want to
                         see her tits. Er… I don't want to see
                         her tits? Do something! I'm
                         panicking here!

MANDY   Shut up yeah!?

ASHLEY   Stop.

            Could be some… wanker.

CARLY   Might be.

            Bet he wishes he was you.

MANDY   David? Give me a mark out of ten.
                         When I do it.

A moment.

CARLY *kisses* ASHLEY.

MANDY *shoots* CARLY *and she falls to the
floor, knocking* ASHLEY*'s beer over.*

The girls cheer.

                         Fuck!

BELLE   Fucking hell Mand, / that was
                         awesome.

MANDY   I got her in the shoulder. Did you see?

ASHLEY *picks up the beer. Drinks it.*

                         David?

DAVID   It was good.

MANDY   No. My *score*. Remember?

DAVID

MANDY

DAVID   Ten.

BELLE   Ten, fuck's sake –

MANDY   Ten! Oh! David! Stop flirting. God.

They giggle. ASHLEY *goes and gets a glass of water. And brings it back to the coffee table by the sofa.*

MANDY *goes up to* DAVID.

You have to tell me how to do it *better.*

Yeah?

How can I improve?

DAVID   Aim for the chest.

MANDY   The chest?

Right.

MANDY *goes back to the gun.*

CARLY *wakes up.*

She moves towards ASHLEY. *She tries to kiss him.*

ASHLEY   What are you doing? We know they're there –

CARLY   I don't give a shit.

ASHLEY   Are you drunk?

CARLY   A bit drunk yeah.

She straddles ASHLEY.

Kisses him. He doesn't really respond.

EMMA   What's wrong with him?

BELLE   Gay.

He just starts to get into it, and MANDY *shoots her again. The girls laugh.*

CARLY *falls awkwardly onto the floor.*

Fucking funny.

ASHLEY *moves her to make her more comfortable.*

EMMA	How many more have we got?
BELLE	Two.
DAVID	You know about the offer then.
BELLE	Yeah we do.
DAVID	I was going to say…
BELLE	Don't need to say anything mate, we already know.
EMMA	Woman said it was only on Wednesdays. Wednesdays are quiet so we get four shots for two.
DAVID	That's right.
BELLE	We know!

They watch.

ASHLEY *walks around the flat a couple of times. Then goes to the fridge and gets another beer. Drinks it. Goes outside.*

DAVID	Sure you two don't want a go?
MANDY	Er. Fuck off.
EMMA	Mandy's birthday. And Belle's drunk.
BELLE	I'd be shit.
DAVID	You?
EMMA	Nah I'm okay.

CARLY *wakes up. Drinks the water.*

Looks unhappy.

ASHLEY stands outside.

They both are still.

BELLE   Can you move her?

David?

It's boring.

Come on.

We've paid.

MANDY   There must be something you can do?

DAVID   I'm sorry.

MANDY   Favour?

For me?

David?

Poke her with a stick or something.

ASHLEY comes back in. Looks at CARLY. He's made a decision.

EMMA   Mand…

ASHLEY takes a swig from his beer.

Then goes to her.

He drinks from the beer.

ASHLEY   They've gone now. No one does more than two.

CARLY   Yeah probably –

He drinks again.

ASHLEY   And even if they haven't, don't care –

                ASHLEY *takes off his T-shirt.*

                Fuck 'em.

EMMA   Oh god, he's going to do her.

ASHLEY   Do it anyway. They can watch.

CARLY   You're sure?

ASHLEY   It's the right time?

CARLY   Yeah but –

ASHLEY   Can't waste it then.

                *He goes to her on the sofa and they start
                kissing again.*

                *He gets on top of her, they fumble to remove
                their clothes.*

                The girls laugh.

BELLE   Is that what your Leo's like when he
                           does you?

EMMA   No.

BELLE   Bet he's shit at it.

EMMA   Er. Shut up?

                ASHLEY *and* CARLY *keep going.*

                The girls watch.

BELLE   I just saw his cock. Not bothered but
                           thought I'd say I did. Cos I did.

                Keep going for a bit, then CARLY *stops.*

CARLY   You okay?

ASHLEY   Yeah. Yeah.

CARLY   Okay.

               They keep going.

               Then once more, CARLY stops, sympathetic –

               Maybe now's not the right –

ASHLEY   *No.* I want to.

EMMA   (*Snigger.*)

               They keep trying.

               Suddenly a sound, and CARLY's shot again.

               MANDY*'s done it. Surprises the other girls.
               They scream.*

BELLE   You're fucking cruel!

               ASHLEY *stops for a moment.*

               Then he tries to keep going.

                      Oh my god! That's rape now. He's
                      actually –

MANDY   Don't think he's actually doing
               anything. / From what she said.

EMMA   He said it was the right time so... he
               must really want a baby.

MANDY   Wouldn't let him.

EMMA   What?

MANDY   People like that. Don't let 'em breed!

               BELLE *bursts out laughing.*

BELLE   Fucking hell...

               ASHLEY *keeps going.*

Look at him. Still going. Uh. Uh.

Leave it mate.

Is that legal?

Stops.

Keeps going again.

Stops.

Come on...

He can't.

Uh.

He gets off and sits on the edge of the sofa out of breath.

EMMA   You've pissed him off.

He looks around for where the shot came from.

Circles the room.

Switches the lights out.

In the dark. He tries to make out faces in the walls, but he can't. Goes to where the girls are. He senses they're there...

MANDY   He can't get out can he?

CARLY *wakes up.*

CARLY   Ashley?

BELLE   Shoot him.

CARLY   What are you doing?

BELLE   Actually. Nah. Shoot her again.
                That's what makes him mental.

He bangs on the wall.

BELLE *bangs back.*

DAVID   Sorry… No… sorry you can't do that.

CARLY   Ashley stop it.

MANDY   They'll kick you out.

BELLE   Like to see them try.

ASHLEY *turns and stares at* CARLY. *Angry.*

CARLY   Ashley…

MANDY   'Ashley'

CARLY   Come here.

MANDY   'Come here'.

He does.

'They're just being horrible'

CARLY   We're alright, aren't we?

She puts her hand out.

He moves towards her, and MANDY *shoots her again.*

She slumps.

ASHLEY *sits on the edge of the sofa.*

DAVID   That's your lot.

BELLE   He could see us. He would've killed you Mand.

MANDY   Not with David protecting us.

DAVID   It was good.

MANDY	What?
DAVID	You… your shooting.
	You did really well.
MANDY	Do you have a girlfriend David?
DAVID	No.
MANDY	Haven't found the right person?
DAVID	…
MANDY	Suppose you're stuck in here all day?
DAVID	…
MANDY	
DAVID	
MANDY	What about me?
	David?
DAVID	You're nice yeah.
MANDY	You think I'm pretty?
DAVID	Yeah.
MANDY	Do you want to take me out then, later?
DAVID	What a –
MANDY	A drink or something?
	No pressure.
DAVID	Okay.
MANDY	Aw.
	Thanks.

But there's just one thing?

You're a bit like my dad?

They go out of the room and burst out laughing.

DAVID *stands in the hide for a moment.*

ASHLEY *stands and looks at where they were.*

DAVID *goes and looks at him in the eyes.*

Some kind of connection.

Scene Five

CARLY *is sat staring out the window.*

DAVID *is in the hide. Waiting. He watches* CARLY.

The door to the hide opens.

It's ASHLEY.

ASHLEY	Hi.
DAVID	Oh…
ASHLEY	You know who I am?
DAVID	Yeah.
ASHLEY	I paid. Saved up and…
DAVID	Right.

Pause.

Come in.

Pause.

I'm David.

ASHLEY	Ashley.
DAVID	Yeah.

He looks out.

You sit here.

ASHLEY   I'm okay. I just want to… look.

He does.

Pause.

How long do I get?

DAVID	Depends on the number of shots.
ASHLEY	One.
DAVID	Twenty minutes.
ASHLEY	That's a long time for just one.

DAVID   It's as much about – sorry – it's
                         weird saying it to you.

ASHLEY

DAVID   The experience is as much about
                         watching and waiting, picking the
                         moment so although it's only one
                         shot, it's important to have the time
                         to choose when you do it.

ASHLEY   You on a shift system?

DAVID   What?

ASHLEY   Different people doing your job. In
                         different places.

DAVID   No, we have our individual locations
                         and that's our responsibility.

ASHLEY   It's always you here then.

DAVID   Normally.

ASHLEY   I didn't know that.

                         So you've seen a lot of us.

DAVID   Yeah.

ASHLEY   Twenty minutes.

DAVID   Eighteen. Do you want to sit down?

                    He does.

                         She's nice.

ASHLEY	What?
DAVID	Carly.

ASHLEY *looks at him.* DAVID *looks at the gun.*

I assume you don't want to –

ASHLEY	What?
DAVID	…
ASHLEY	
DAVID	Right.

ASHLEY *looks at him again. Stands up.*

ASHLEY	I… You've been watching us, you know we want kids, you know about that.
DAVID	Look –
ASHLEY	You know all that, right?
DAVID	Yeah.
ASHLEY	Yeah. And… okay. So you've also seen, in the last few weeks, last couple of months, now it could be any time, that, I've, it's been difficult for me, for us. To.
	Shit you know what I'm saying. I don't have to say it.
DAVID	Yeah.
ASHLEY	But now I've paid, I'm the only one looking in at our house, yes?
DAVID	Yes.
ASHLEY	So can you just, leave me to it?

DAVID	What?
ASHLEY	I'll go back to the house, with Carly, and you step out, just step out of here for twenty minutes and –
DAVID	Sixteen.
ASHLEY	Alright, for sixteen minutes you step out and leave us to it.
DAVID	Look –
ASHLEY	Then I'd know. It was just.
DAVID	I can't – you're the client, you've paid, I've got to accompany you, I can't leave you with her –
ASHLEY	She's my wife.
DAVID	I know but you've paid now for this, I have to supervise –
ASHLEY	Come on.
DAVID	It's my job.
ASHLEY	Mate.
DAVID	It's my job. I can't lose my job. You get that. I can't lose my job.
ASHLEY	Right.

DAVID	I could just not watch.
ASHLEY	What?
DAVID	I have to stay in here, officially make sure you're okay, but I could just turn the other way.

Pause.

ASHLEY   How would I know?

DAVID   What?

ASHLEY   That you had.

DAVID   ...I would.

ASHLEY   But I don't know you, how do I
                know you'd not be watching?

DAVID   I... promise. I'll look away.

ASHLEY   Okay. Okay. Yeah. Thanks...

                He goes.

                A moment.

                Then the front door of the house opens, and
                ASHLEY *enters.*

CARLY   Where were you? I was upstairs. Come down
                and you're not here.

ASHLEY   I went for a walk.

CARLY   Why? Not like you.

ASHLEY   Okay, I just –

CARLY   I thought you might have gone.

ASHLEY   Gone where.

CARLY   Gone.

                A moment.

                ASHLEY *looks out at the hide.*

                Then he walks to her.

In the hide, DAVID *watches for a moment,
then turns the other way round, on his own.*

ASHLEY *goes over and kisses* CARLY,
passionately.

She laughs. Responds.

Behind DAVID, ASHLEY *and* CARLY *start
to have sex.*

Scene Six

Seven years later.

Everything looks older.

DAVID *is watching from the hide with* MARGARET.

LIAM *opens a wrapped-up present.* ASHLEY *and* CARLY *watch. When he speaks, it's very quietly.*

MARGARET   He's got that look.

DAVID   What?

                  LIAM *continues unwrapping.*

MARGARET   Take a load of kids, you can tell
                  instantly which ones are going to
                  jail. You can see it. The eyes.

                  LIAM *finishes opening it. It's a PlayStation
                  Vita.*

CARLY   Is that the one?

ASHLEY   Yeah it is. Right?

MARGARET   Armed robbery...

CARLY   Is it?

LIAM   Yeah.

MARGARET   Assault. Rape. I always know.

                  LIAM *quickly starts opening up the box,
                  switching it on.* ASHLEY *and* CARLY *watch.*

                  Even when they're nine years old,
                  there's something in the look.
                  Something psychopathic, you're
                  standing up there in front of the
                  class and you can tell in a class of
                  thirty, there's always a couple.

The game springs to life. Noise. Graphics.

CARLY   We had a Master System.

ASHLEY   Sega.

CARLY   Yeah.

MARGARET   Anywhere is it?

DAVID   Well no. Not in the head. And not on
                           the stairs.

MARGARET   Of course. I mean anywhere that I
                           normally shoot an adult.

DAVID   Yes. The same.

                She settles to take the shot.

                           But don't.

MARGARET   What?

DAVID   Don't be cruel.

MARGARET   Don't be cruel. Is that a
                           Is that official?

DAVID   No.

MARGARET   Something I have to listen to?

ASHLEY   You played this before.

LIAM   Yeah.

MARGARET   You know what this is?

ASHLEY   On your friend's one?

LIAM   / Yeah.

MARGARET   I mean you work here. Jesus, you
                           advertise this big new thing, with the
                           kids, then when we turn up, what?
                           You get squeamish.

DAVID   Sorry.

                CARLY goes and gets a glass of water.

MARGARET   Supposed to be a unique experience.
                        Supposed to be hosted by experts.
                        A day you'll never forget. Not quite
                        that is it?

ASHLEY   Can you get me a Coke?

                CARLY *gets a Coke from the fridge.*

MARGARET   'Don't be cruel.'

                        You need training.

                        They say you're struggling you lot. I
                        can see why.

                CARLY *comes back with the Coke for*
                ASHLEY *and the water, which she puts on*
                the table.

                        My friend Casey, works in primary,
                        she says it's in a name.

                        She says if they're called Callum,
                        Connor, Liam, Daniel... forget it.

                        Darren.

                        Gary.

                        What's your name?

DAVID   David.

MARGARET   Ah well. Yes. See? You're a good boy.

                        Never any trouble from you.

CARLY   You okay?

ASHLEY   Don't know.

                MARGARET *settles to take the shot.*

MARGARET   What's he called?

DAVID   Liam.

MARGARET smiles.

MARGARET   Well. There you are. Exactly what I
                    said.

She lines up the sights.

DAVID   So just take your time, settle and let
                    your –

*MARGARET shoots LIAM and he slumps on
the chair.*

CARLY   Fuck. Fuck.

*ASHLEY and CARLY go to him and lie him
down.*

Okay. Fuck. No. We're not doing this.

I can't.

MARGARET   It's not that different.

CARLY   Ashley? I'm telling you. / It's a mistake.

MARGARET   Done loads of these over the years –

ASHLEY   Fine. / I know.

MARGARET   – got boring to be honest, when they
                    said kids, / I thought that might spice
                    things up but...

CARLY   Don't care what they say.

MARGARET   No.

CARLY   If they're saying we have to do this or leave
                    then we'll leave.

MARGARET   Dull.

CARLY   It's not worth it.

ASHLEY   Yeah. Okay. Okay. I know.

CARLY	Fuck.
ASHLEY	We said we'd try. And we have. We don't like it. Now we know.
CARLY	Yeah.

CARLY *sits with him.* ASHLEY *picks up the game and pauses it.*

MARGARET	You don't have children?
DAVID	No.
MARGARET	Why not?
DAVID	…

ASHLEY *goes to the fridge and gets a can of Coke. Opens it and brings it back.*

MARGARET	Got a girlfriend?
DAVID	I was in the army for –
MARGARET	Gay?
DAVID	No.
MARGARET	What then? Never wanted them?
DAVID	It just… hasn't happened.
MARGARET	Well whatever the reason, good.
	Too many of them as it is.
ASHLEY	He's alright.
	Look.
MARGARET	This way out is it?
DAVID	Yeah.
MARGARET	Right.

LIAM *comes round and looks at them.*

ASHLEY   You alright?

              LIAM *looks confused.*

              How about a Coke? You must be thirsty.

              LIAM *drinks from the can.*

              That's it.

CARLY   Not doing it again.

ASHLEY   No.

              A moment, then LIAM *reaches for his game.*
              Picks it up and goes and sits on the sofa,
              playing it.

              CARLY *and* ASHLEY *look at each other.*
              He's alright…

Scene Seven

DAVID *and* SARAH *are in the hide.*

LIAM *is on the mezzanine level, playing on the computer game, sat inside a large cardboard box.* CARLY *is standing with him. She tries to lift it but* LIAM *holds it down.*

ASHLEY *is sat on the sofa downstairs.*

CARLY *tries again.*

CARLY	Stop it.
	Once more – this time much harder – a struggle, but LIAM *stays inside the box.*
	CARLY *looks at it for a moment.*
	Then comes downstairs. A glance at ASHLEY.
	She goes into the kitchen.
	Opens a drawer.
	Takes out some scissors and heads upstairs.
ASHLEY	Carly.
CARLY	What?
ASHLEY	You can't use *scissors.*
CARLY	What then?
	CARLY *gets no reply from* ASHLEY *so goes back into the kitchen.*
	Puts the scissors away.
	She goes to the fridge and gets out a lasagne for one, unwraps it.
	She puts it in the microwave and switches it on. Waits.
SARAH	You've been running with complete families for a while.

DAVID	Must be... four months.
SARAH	What about employment legislation?
DAVID	Maybe you should talk to –
SARAH	You can't have children working.
DAVID	Officially they're not working.
SARAH	No?
DAVID	Performing.
SARAH	Good.
DAVID	That's what we're told to say.
SARAH	Yes. Well remembered.
	Not performing today, is he?
DAVID	He's shy.
SARAH	I've got one myself. Just like this. Says she loves ballet then she won't get on stage.

Pause.

	Did you get a say when they expanded. When they started to bring children into it?
DAVID	No. Well, they had to. This was the first – but these days – those new reserves – apparently there's a whole village with a gun on a jeep –
SARAH	So it was a response to the competition.
DAVID	I suppose.
SARAH	But did they give you a choice, did they ask you what you think? About the children.

DAVID	No.
CARLY	There are times when I want to get in a box.

The microwave pings. She takes the lasagne out.

But I don't, do I?

SARAH	Do you think there's a line David?
DAVID	What?
SARAH	Between doing this with consenting adults and children.
DAVID	Yes. Probably.

CARLY takes the lasagne out of the plastic and puts it on a plate.

SARAH	That's not what you should say.
DAVID	Oh. You were –
SARAH	You need to be careful.
DAVID	I wasn't sure if you were asking me really or as a –
SARAH	Yes, that's why I'm here, with eight outstanding cases already, all employees need to know how to answer the question. The fact is, thinking about this stuff isn't your job – the ethics and morals – is it? It's your job to make it safe. So if someone asks if you think there's an ethical line, you just need to say that it's not up to you.
DAVID	Yeah.

CARLY takes the lasagne upstairs and puts it by the box.

SARAH   In fact if a question starts 'do you think', you don't have to answer it. The law is about facts, and they know that so they would have to rephrase the question – Have you seen any evidence that this practice causes harm to the children concerned? What would you answer to that?

CARLY   I've got lasagne.

Right here if you come out.

DAVID   No. I haven't seen any evidence.

SARAH   Good.

ASHLEY   We were going to have two.

CARLY   *What?*

ASHLEY   Jack and Missy.

Beat.

CARLY   Ashley come and help me or shut the fuck up.

SARAH   Are they close?

DAVID   Close?

SARAH   The family?

DAVID   Yeah. They're okay.

SARAH   What's the boy like?

DAVID   Well he's a little boy isn't he? Does stupid things. Likes computer games.

SARAH   What sort?

DAVID   Boys' ones. Fighting.

SARAH   What do you make of that?

DAVID		Doesn't do any harm.
SARAH		You were a soldier. You saw real guns. Fighting. Injuries.
		So what do you think?
DAVID		It's just a game.
SARAH		No.
DAVID		What?
SARAH		I asked you what you think.
	Beat.	
DAVID		That's not my job.
SARAH		Good.
CARLY	Liam.	
SARAH		Why's he hiding in a box?
DAVID		He's scared.
SARAH		Do you know that?
DAVID		It's obvious.
SARAH		What's the evidence?
DAVID		That he's in there.
SARAH		He could just be playing? He could be annoying his mum. He might be loving it. You don't know he's scared do you? So why's he hiding in the box?
DAVID		I'm not –
SARAH		Are you a psychologist?
DAVID		
SARAH		Do you have any clinical evidence?

DAVID	No.
SARAH	So do you know for sure why's he hiding in the box?
DAVID	No
SARAH	So why's he hiding in the box?
DAVID	I don't know.
SARAH	Good.

CARLY tries to lift the box. LIAM makes a noise as he tries to stop her.

ASHLEY   Leave him.

She keeps trying.

CARLY   There are worse things people do, to live.

ASHLEY   He doesn't want to.

She gives up again, furious now.

CARLY   Okay he doesn't want to, so we get kicked out, he gets kicked out of his school, we don't have a house we live somewhere shit, like where Mum lives, and he goes to your old school instead, and that was bad then, worse now, what do you think is going to happen to him there as he gets older? You think he's safer there?

ASHLEY   I did alright.

CARLY   You did not. Fucking. Do alright. Ashley. You didn't.

Suddenly ASHLEY stands up, storms upstairs and rips the box off LIAM.

SARAH   Here we go.

LIAM makes a sound, and as the box crashes across the room, we find LIAM, in a hoodie,

with the hood pulled down over his face.
ASHLEY holds LIAM and pulls at his hood.

ASHLEY   Take it off.

                Fucking...

CARLY   Liam...

                ASHLEY pulls harder. Struggles with LIAM.
                It's messy.

                ASHLEY pulls LIAM's hood off his face and
                holds it.

SARAH   Could you shoot him yourself?

DAVID   If I had to.

SARAH   It would be useful if we knew you
                            had no qualms yourself.

                            If you could get up and state that.

                DAVID picks up the gun.

ASHLEY   Open your eyes.

                Open your eyes.

                LIAM stands in the room with his eyes
                closed.

                DAVID shoots. LIAM falls to the ground.

                ASHLEY sits on the floor and waits. Out of
                breath.

                A moment.

                ASHLEY goes and gets some water. Brings it
                back.

DAVID   It's not normally like this.

                LIAM wakes up. ASHLEY goes to give
                LIAM his water.

He stops. LIAM *has moved away and is staring straight at* ASHLEY.

SARAH   It's… David isn't it?

DAVID   Yeah.

SARAH   Right.

Scene Eight

LIAM *is in his box – which has now moved to a corner of the room.* CARLY *is with him. Sat next to the box on the floor.*

JOHN *is in the hide watching, drunk, eating crisps.*

This goes on for a long time.

Eventually CARLY *dims the light.*

We see that LIAM *has a torch inside the box.*

DAVID *enters the hide, not expecting* JOHN.

DAVID	Oh.

They look at each other.

JOHN	I do own it David.
DAVID	What?
JOHN	I am allowed to be here.
DAVID	Course.
	Just. Didn't expect you. It's not –
JOHN	It's this family isn't it?
DAVID	That…
JOHN	That you know so much about.
DAVID	They asked if I was concerned about any of them. I answered the questions truthfully. I was under oath.

JOHN	Yeah okay, look, I don't mind David. It warmed my cold fucking heart, your story. Really *touching*.
DAVID	I just answered the questions.
JOHN	Yeah and we just lost one point three million in collective damages.
DAVID	I'm on my way home.
	Locking up.
JOHN	Sit down.

JOHN is distracted by ASHLEY *coming back in the front door, wearing an ill-fitting suit.*

He kisses CARLY.

ASHLEY	(*Referring to* LIAM.) Has he…
CARLY	No.
	You're late.
ASHLEY	The car stopped working. Called the number. They said that benefit had been withdrawn. Told me to leave the car where it was.
	Got the bus back.

JOHN *offers* DAVID *a drink.*

JOHN	Sit down.
DAVID	No thanks.
JOHN	I'm your boss. Have a fucking drink.
DAVID	Right.
JOHN	Got some crisps too. Pringles.

ASHLEY *gets a beer and sits down.*

CARLY	You don't look well.

ASHLEY   You go in and they see you and you do the
          whole interview then they always eventually
          say they don't think this is right for you at this
          stage, and you know what they mean.

JOHN   You think I've been nasty. You think
              I'm a bad person.

DAVID   No.

JOHN   Giving them a house and a living.

DAVID   I didn't say that.

JOHN   An income.

DAVID   No.

JOHN   You think I should feel some kind of
              responsibility to these people?

              That's what everyone else thinks.
              Now we're scaling back, shutting
              down, I'm supposed to get them jobs
              as well. What do you think about
              that?

DAVID

JOHN   Well? What do you think?

DAVID   I don't know.

ASHLEY   Today was better.

JOHN   They're adults David.

              They're not stupid.

              They knew what this was. They
              milked it for all it was worth.
              Now I'm supposed to help them.

ASHLEY   They said they might have something in a
          couple of weeks. They'd keep me in mind.

CARLY   Doing what?

ASHLEY   Data entry.

JOHN   Actually. Scratch that. Maybe they
                are. Maybe they are just really stupid.

CARLY   How much?

ASHLEY   Seven pounds an hour.

JOHN   What's next?

DAVID   You mean…

JOHN   We shot the men, we shot the
                women, we shot the kids. We're still
                not making the money we used to.
                So what's next?

                That's what we need David. The next
                idea.

ASHLEY   It's a start.

CARLY   Is it?

ASHLEY   It would mean we could think about finding
                somewhere else –

CARLY   Seven pounds an hour. There are three of us.

ASHLEY   It's a start.

JOHN   I think we should make it hurt.

DAVID   I'm sorry?

JOHN   Make them actually suffer. Charge
                more. Punters would love that.

                If this was Holland we could do
                euthanasia.

                I should look into that.

                What do you think?

                Put people out of their misery.

                Pop.

	There's a market.
	People would pay.
	It might work.
DAVID	I...
	I don't think it...
JOHN	I'm joking.
ASHLEY	You go out and find something then.
JOHN	You really don't laugh do you?
	Go on.
	Smile now.
ASHLEY	See if you can do better.
JOHN	They write me letters.
	Say I earn too much.
	I'm like fuck off.
ASHLEY	What?
JOHN	You didn't take the risk, find the investment, develop the technology, mortgage your own house in the first place. You didn't have the idea. What have you done? Sit there. Ask for everything on a fucking plate. Now you're writing letters. Well fuck you.
CARLY	I don't want to say it Ashley, I don't want to say it out loud because really it's so depressing.

JOHN *picks up the gun.*

JOHN	They've had every opportunity. They're lucky.
ASHLEY	What? What?

CARLY	When they said they'd keep you in mind it was just a nicer way of getting you out the room, it was easier for them to say that, easier in the moment but –
ASHLEY	
CARLY	They won't call. It's not different to the others.
ASHLEY	Yes, it is, listen.
CARLY	No –
ASHLEY	I think he could tell I was –
CARLY	He was being polite there's no way he was going to give you a job, after being in here all this time neither of us is going to –

JOHN *shoots* CARLY, *and then immediately* ASHLEY. *He falls to the ground.*

JOHN	That's / better.
DAVID	Sorry. Sorry. You can't –
JOHN	Well they can sue me then, can't they? They can join the queue.
	Thank god most of them can't afford it.
	Look at her.
	They were supposed to be attractive. Originally. Look what happened. Fucking metaphor for the whole thing she is.
	Chubby fucking…
	Surprised the darts work.
	Need an elephant gun.
	Ten bore.

A moment.

JOHN *shoots them both again.*

JOHN *laughs.*

DAVID	That's a double dose.
JOHN	'Double dose'
DAVID	Give it to me.
JOHN	Uh... uh... 'okay okay'

Twitching.

'The rules.'

I wrote the rules.

What do you do?

Here?

When there's no customers.

You just wait? Or something.

What do you do?

What do you do at home?

Where do you live? Is it a flat? I bet it's a little flat, and you have everything in the right place. Just in exactly the precise position it should be.

A simple life.

Ever invite people home?

Ever meet anyone?

Phone ever ring?

DAVID   None of your fucking business.

JOHN *smiles and gives him the gun back.*

JOHN   So you know.

We filed today.

In two weeks, we'll all be out. You.

Me.

Them.

It's over.

Thank god.

He leaves.

DAVID *stays and watches.*

CARLY *wakes up again.*

ASHLEY *wakes up again.*

He sits down, and stares, facing away from her.

She looks at him.

DAVID *goes right up to the screen of the hide.*

Scene Nine

The flat is back to its original state – but with some wear and tear.

CARLY *is stood in the middle of the living room, in her coat.*

There is a small cardboard box on the floor with their stuff in.

LIAM *is in his box, now on the mezzanine level, playing the computer game.*

ASHLEY *comes down the stairs holding a couple of DVDs. He's slightly vague. Wearing a rucksack.*

ASHLEY	Always something else.
	Back of the cupboard.
	He puts it in the box.
	CARLY *looks at* ASHLEY.
CARLY	You need to put your coat on first.
	They said it was raining. Not here. Not yet.
	Might be walking round a lot today.
ASHLEY	Distracted.
CARLY	Yeah.
ASHLEY	Sorry.
	She picks up his coat.
	Takes the rucksack off him.
	He puts his coat on.
	Puts the rucksack back over.
CARLY	Did you speak to him?
ASHLEY	I tried but – I told him this morning. Said we were off. He does know.
CARLY	Found my old phone.

ASHLEY   Good. Thought you would've thrown it away
                threw mine away. So did you try –

CARLY   Yeah I tried Fiona but the number doesn't
                work. She must've changed it. Probably
                changed it ages ago.

                We should go.

ASHLEY   Yeah.

                ASHLEY *goes to the fridge. Opens it.*

                Takes out a small piece of cheese.

                Eats it.

CARLY   Ashley we should go.

ASHLEY   I told him. That it was today.

                I don't know if he listens any more.

CARLY   What do you think we should do? We can't
                miss this bus.

ASHLEY   I did say.

                I told him.

                CARLY *looks upstairs.*

                ASHLEY *goes upstairs.*

                He looks at the box.

                Liam.

                Liam.

                We have to go.

He lifts the box – LIAM kicks out, grabs the box, and gets back inside.

ASHLEY watches for a moment.

Then comes back down the stairs.

CARLY shouts to him.

CARLY   Liam, if you don't come now, you'll never see us again. We'll leave you behind and we don't know where we're going.

So you need to come out.

Liam.

Liam.

Okay

We're going then.

ASHLEY   He knows we won't.

They wait.

Jamie. We could try Jamie.

CARLY   Who?

ASHLEY   He's a mate. From school.

CARLY   Got his number?

ASHLEY   …

A knock on the door.

CARLY opens it. It's DAVID.

DAVID	Hi… I'm David. Your warden. Can I come in?
CARLY	You're here for the…
DAVID	I…
CARLY	The inventory is it?
DAVID	Right.

He comes in. Sees ASHLEY.

	Hi.
ASHLEY	Hi.
DAVID	David.
ASHLEY	Good to meet you.
CARLY	That's ours. That's our stuff there.
	And there's Liam.
	The furniture and everything's that's left, that's all yours.
	We've got till eleven.
	They said…
DAVID	Yes it's fine.
	I'm just…
	I…
	It looks strange doesn't it?
	Like this.
ASHLEY	
CARLY	What?
DAVID	Liam's upstairs?
ASHLEY	There.
DAVID	Does he still have his game?

CARLY	We thought you wouldn't mind him keeping that. It's old now. I know it's not ours but… We thought you wouldn't mind.
DAVID	It's on the list actually.
CARLY	You're joking.
DAVID	Yes.
CARLY	Oh.
DAVID	It's fine. He can keep it.
	Where are you going?
ASHLEY	We're going to try friends.
CARLY	What do you want?
DAVID	
CARLY	
DAVID	You're getting the eleven o'clock bus?
ASHLEY	Yeah.
DAVID	You should go then.
CARLY	We know.
DAVID	You should leave by ten thirty if you're walking up to the road.
CARLY	Yeah.
ASHLEY	We'll be alright.
CARLY	It's Liam. He doesn't want to come out.
DAVID	There's only one bus. Shall I have a word. With Liam?

ASHLEY   He's our son, if we can't –

CARLY   Yeah.

              Why not?

              DAVID *goes upstairs to the mezzanine level.*
              ASHLEY *and* CARLY *watch.*

              DAVID *looks at the box for a minute.*
              He sits down next to the box.

              Close to it.

              Speaks quietly.

DAVID   Hello

              Soldier?

              You're sat in the dark and you want to be
              safe. That's good. That makes sense. You're
              bright. You're a bright boy.

              But you've got to make a decision.

              You can stay in there and see what happens.
              Or you can come out.

              It's up to you.

              If you come out it won't be easy.

You understand?

You'll have to go and play football when it's cold, and you don't want to.

You'll have to make new friends with horrible people.

Watch films you hate.

You'll have to go to school every day, and pretend you know the answers when you don't.

Then you're going to have to meet girls and that'll be difficult for ever, that never gets easy. Then you won't know what to do, and everyone else will seem to breeze through it while you can't do the easiest things and it won't be fair, won't ever be fair, you'll struggle to get a house, struggle to get a job that doesn't make you feel like shit. And when you do find it, it won't last for ever, and then you'll be back out there again, older, and less useful. You might have kids and have to look after them, or you might not but either way it'll be difficult all of it, all the time, it'll be really really hard.

But it's either facing all that, or staying in there.

Those are your options.

So?

Soldier.

Liam?

What do you think?

I'm still here.

What do you think?

Soldier?

LIAM *throws the box off.*

Sits in front of DAVID *with his hood down.*

Good boy.

Now how you doing?

Look at me.

Look at me soldier.

He looks up.

Give me the game.

LIAM *gives him the game.*

DAVID *puts the coat and the bag on* LIAM.

You've been very brave.

To go out there and do all that. To step outside and face all that.

You must be much more brave than I can even imagine.

LIAM *goes and holds* CARLY*'s hand.*

CARLY *looks at* DAVID, *still sat on the floor. Astonished.*

You should go.

They leave.

DAVID *comes down the stairs.*

He reaches across to his bag.

Takes out a tranquiliser gun.

Puts a dart in the gun.

Sits on the stairs.

Puts the end of the gun in his mouth.

Pulls the trigger.

He convulses for a few seconds.

He dies.

End.

www.nickhernbooks.co.uk

facebook.com/nickhernbooks

twitter.com/nickhernbooks